From Highs To Healing

Unraveling the Psychological Effects of Drug Addiction on Youth

Stefan Frey

Table of contents

Preface   **4**

Purpose and Scope   6

INTRODUCTION   **8**

Brief history of drug use   8

The Youth and Substance Use   10

CHAPTER 1   **13**

THE ALLURE OF HIGHS   **13**

Psychological Triggers for Drug Use   13

CHAPTER 2   **16**

MARIJUANA AND THE MIND   **16**

Cognitive Consequences for Adolescents   16

CHAPTER 3   **19**

TRAMADOL'S TRAP   **19**

Emotional Turmoil and Dependency   19

CHAPTER 4   **22**

BEYOND COMMON SUBSTANCES   **22**

Lesser-Known Drugs and Their Psychological Impact   22

CHAPTER 5   **26**

THE DOWNWARD SPIRAL   **26**

Addiction and Mental Health Disorders   26

CHAPTER 6   **29**

BREAKING FREE   **29**

Psychological Approaches to Recovery   29

CHAPTER 7   **32**
COMMUNITY AND SUPPORT   **32**
     The Role of Peers and Family in Healing   32
CHAPTER 8   **35**
A NEW DAWN   **35**
     Life Beyond Addiction   35
CONCLUSION   **38**
     Setting Out for a Better Future   38
     Acknowledgements   40

Preface

Every youth has a universe of possibilities inside of them, a blank canvas ready to be filled with the vivid hues of their goals and desires. However, drug abuse casts a shadow over this canvas for others, a problem that may ruin even the most promising prospects.

The urgent necessity to address this developing problem gave rise to this book. It serves as a ray of hope and a manual for those who are entangled in the web of addiction, either individually or via loved ones. This is especially true for narcotics like marijuana and tramadol, which are increasingly common among young people.

This book is a tour through young people's thoughts, examining the many ways that drugs may change their psychological environment. It is not only a collection of scientific data and psychological beliefs. By exploring the psychological and cognitive impacts that might result in reliance, this story aims to explain the "why" behind drug use and addiction.

This book also serves as a container for answers. In order to navigate the maze of addiction, it provides helpful guidance, research-backed tactics, and sincere support. It addresses adolescents directly, providing them with the information and resources they need to take back control of their life and chart a path toward resilience and recovery.

I pray that as you read these pages, you will discover strength when you are weak, clarity when you are confused, and most importantly, a way out of the darkest places of reliance and onto the pinnacle of recovery.

Welcome to a transformative trip.

Purpose and Scope

Highlighting the complex psychological struggles that young people caught in the cycle of drug addiction confront is the main goal of this book With a focus on drugs like tramadol, marijuana, and other common narcotics among young people, this book aims to analyze the psychological and emotional effects of substance usage.

We go beyond just naming issues; our investigation is a thorough manual that provides practical fixes and youth-oriented tactics. The range of this book includes:

Understanding Addiction: Examining the psychological factors, such as social pressures, emotional anguish, and mental health conditions, that lead young people to resort to drugs.

Impacts on the Developing Mind: focusing on the effects that drugs like marijuana and tramadol have on the growing brains of young adults and adolescents.

Routes that Lead to Dependency underlying psychological patterns and triggers while identifying the steps that lead from occasional usage to addiction.

Options for Recuperation: offering evidence-based psychiatric treatments, systems of community support, and techniques for personal development to fight addiction.

Prevention: Talking about how to provide young people the knowledge and skills they need to make responsible choices about using drugs.

The target audience for this book is not just the young people themselves, but also educators, parents, and mental health experts. It is a call to action to educate people about the psychological effects of drug addiction and to provide our children with the information and resources they need to live healthy, drug-free lives.

Brief history of drug use

The history of drugs and drug usage is as ancient as civilization. Drugs have long been a component of human culture, from the usage of opium poppies by the ancient Sumerians to the problems with synthetic compounds today. We go on a historical tour to comprehend the development of drug usage and its effects on young people in this book.

"Discovery's Early Years" The first evidence of drug usage dates back to Mesopotamian Sumerians who planted and harvested opium poppies, often known as "joy plants," about 3400 B.C. Opium proliferated with the expansion of trade channels, ultimately making its way to Egypt, Persia, and Europe.

Combining Cultures: Several societies have included drug usage into their ceremonies and medicinal practices throughout history. While the Chinese utilized cannabis in their medicinal procedures, the Greeks used opium to relieve pain. Native Americans in the Americas used hallucinogenic herbs, such as peyote, for spiritual reasons.

The Increase in Leisure Use The 19th century saw a change in the direction of recreational drug usage. Opium dens spread from Asia to the West. The introduction of novel administration techniques with the development of the hypodermic needle in 1853 raised the risk of addiction.

Limitations and Supervision With the signing of the International Opium Convention in 1912, drug prohibition laws were first implemented in the early 20th century. A number of chemicals were made illegal in the next decades, which paved the way for the "war on drugs" in the 1970s.

Contemporary Difficulties Today's adolescents must navigate a world in which new and synthetic psychoactive substances coexist with established ones like marijuana and tramadol. The dynamics of drug culture have shifted as a result of the internet and social media, which have increased accessibility to drugs and modified perceptions of their usage.

The goal of this book is to provide young people a thorough grasp of the psychological impacts of drug addiction. It will examine the background information, the motivations for drug use, and the effects on mental health. Most importantly, it will provide tactics and answers to assist young people in navigating the murky waters of drug misuse and determining how to get treatment.

The Youth and Substance Use

In today's world, young people using drugs is a complicated phenomena entwined with themes of stress, curiosity, rebellion, and identity exploration. By exposing the patterns that guide young people into drug use and addiction, "From Highs To Healing " seeks to disentangle this tapestry.

The Period of Field Trials A person's drive to discover new things often clashes with the process of developing an individual identity throughout their formative years as a young person. The natural tendency to experiment with drugs like tramadol, marijuana, and other substances is characteristic of this stage of life.

Impacts of Society: Adolescents' opinions toward drugs are greatly influenced by their peer group. Young people may be influenced to make decisions that are in line with their friends' preferences, sometimes at the price of their own wellbeing, by their urge to fit in and their fear of losing out.

Coping strategies with stress: Teenagers may experience elevated stress levels due to social demands, scholastic achievement expectations, and future uncertainties. Oftentimes, people mistake drugs for a fast way out of these situations, providing just fleeting solace but with long-term psychological repercussions.

Impact of the Digital Age Substance usage has taken on new dimensions with the development of the internet and social media. More people than ever have access to information on drugs, and the way drugs are portrayed in digital media may mainstream and glamorize drug use, which can have a negative impact on young people's brains.

Inside the Mind's Maze Although using drugs or alcohol may first seem innocuous, it may soon spiral into a maze of psychological dependence. Drugs may change mood, cognition, and behavior, which can start an addiction cycle in young people whose growing brains are especially vulnerable to their effects.

Moving in the Direction of Answers Along with highlighting the problems, this book aims to provide a path forward for finding answers. It will include information on therapeutic treatments, support networks, and successful preventative tactics that help steer young people away from drug abuse and toward a happier, healthier existence.

The psychological impacts of certain substances, the phases of addiction, and the recovery process will all be covered in more detail in the next chapters. Giving young people the tools and information they need to overcome the obstacles posed by drug addiction and help them create resilient futures is our mission.

The complicated problem of teenage substance abuse is introduced in this part, which also lays the groundwork for a more thorough examination of the psychological ramifications of drug addiction and the strategies that may support the recovery and well-being of young people. It gives a basis for comprehending the circumstances around drug use and the need of taking a holistic approach to tackling this problem.

CHAPTER 1

THE ALLURE OF HIGHS

Psychological Triggers for Drug Use

The Search for Happiness One of the basic human drives is the desire for pleasure, and drugs provide an easy way to achieve strong emotions of euphoria. Substances take over the brain's reward system, giving pleasure-related neurotransmitters like dopamine an artificial boost.

Get Away from Reality Drugs are a common way for young people to escape the stresses of everyday life. Whether it's familial problems, personal concerns, or school-related stress, narcotics may provide a brief escape from reality and a perilous delusion of comfort.

The Requirement for Acceptance in Society Adolescence is a time when the need to blend in and be accepted by peers is a strong drive. When drug use is common in a social group, young people may take drugs as a social lubricant because they feel too much pressure to fit in.

Curiosity and Trial and error: Youth is a time when innate curiosity and the desire to try new things are enhanced. Drugs may be especially alluring to young people due to its mystery and taboo, which might lead them to explore without fully comprehending the dangers.

Self-Caregivers for Mental Well-Being Some young people may resort to drugs as a kind of self-medication for undiagnosed or untreated mental health conditions, such as anxiety or depression, in the lack of appropriate mental health assistance.

Managing Trauma: Drugs may become a coping technique for trauma survivors, helping them to forget their agony. But this kind of self-medication may easily turn into addiction and dependence.

Pop Culture and the Media's Effect Drug use is often glamorized in the media and popular culture, which presents it as a normal and even desirable activity. A young person's view of drugs may be distorted by this representation, which minimizes the dangers and repercussions.

Recognizing the Triggers, Effective preventative measures begin with an understanding of these psychological factors. We can better prepare young people to resist the attraction of highs and make healthier decisions by addressing the root causes of drug use.

The particular psychological impacts of drugs like marijuana and tramadol on young people will be discussed in detail in the parts that follow, along with strategies for guiding them away from addiction and toward a more promising future free of drugs.

CHAPTER 2

MARIJUANA AND THE MIND

Cognitive Consequences for Adolescents

Understanding the effects of marijuana on the growing brain becomes essential as we dive further into the cognitive landscape of adolescence. In "From Highs To Healing ," Here we will explore the complex connection between marijuana use and adolescent cognitive development.

The Adolescent Brain in Development
The developing teenage brain is a work in progress that is going through major changes. The development of critical regions related to risk assessment, emotional control, and decision-making makes teenagers more susceptible to the negative effects of psychoactive drugs like marijuana.

1.Immediate cognitive deficits brought on by marijuana consumption include
Memory: Having trouble remembering things and creating new ones.
Attention: A diminished capacity to concentrate and maintain concentration on tasks.

Judgment: Poor decision-making skills that result in unsafe actions.

2.Prolonged Cognitive Repercussions Adolescents who use marijuana regularly may see long-term repercussions on their cognitive abilities.

Neurodevelopmental Delay: A possible barrier to the growth of analytical and problem-solving abilities.
Learning impairments include difficulties remembering new knowledge and doing well academically.

Modified Brain Structure: Modifications to the gray matter of the brain, especially in regions related to learning and memory.

Dependency on Psychology Cannabis' psychological appeal may result in reliance, a condition in which a user's mental and emotional well-being becomes more and more dependent on the substance in order to feel "normal" or "happy."

3.Effects on Emotional Well-Being
Studies reveal a link between marijuana usage and the escalation of mental health conditions like.

Anxiety: Increased apprehension and suspicion.

Depression: Enhanced vulnerability to mood disorders and depressed symptoms
.

Psychosis: Heavy usage has the potential to sometimes set up psychotic episodes.

4.Managing the Risks

It is essential to comprehend these cognitive effects in order to create treatments and preventative strategies. Among the solutions are:

Education: Teaching young people the dangers of marijuana usage.

Counseling: Offering assistance to those who are battling addiction.

Healthy Substitutes: Supporting pursuits that enhance mental and emotional health.

Marijuana usage throughout adolescence has significant and varied cognitive effects. We can assist young people in making choices that prioritize their cognitive health and general well-being by tackling these problems head-on and providing workable answers.

CHAPTER 3

TRAMADOL'S TRAP

Emotional Turmoil and Dependency

Tramadol often has a misleading role in the story of drug addiction. Although it is marketed as a less dangerous substitute for other opioids, improper use of it may plunge young people into a maze of psychological problems and dependence.

The Erroneous View of Safety Because of its legal status and authorized usage for pain relief from moderate to severe pain, tramadol is frequently seen as a safe medicine. This idea may give young people a false feeling of security and raise their risk of abuse.

When Emotional Dependency Begins Not only does tramadol relieve physical pain, but it also momentarily eases mental anguish. Tramadol users who depend on medication to deal with everyday stressors and emotional difficulties risk turning this dual alleviation into an emotional crutch very rapidly.

The Dependency Cycle Young people may find themselves in a loop of increased dose and frequency of tramadol use as their tolerance to its effects grows. Because of the drug's disruption of the brain's natural reward system, users may become emotionally dependent on it and become obsessed with obtaining its soothing benefits.

The Slippage Into Emotional Chaos Misuse of tramadol may have negative side effects that make emotional instability worse.

Users could encounter

1.Mood swings: Sudden, erratic shifts in mood.

2.Anxiety: Increased anxiety, especially when there is no purpose.

3.Depression: A feeling of hopelessness and sadness that grows.

4.The Effect of Isolation
Tramadol addiction may cause social disengagement because individuals put their drug usage above their relationships and social life. The emotional upheaval and healing attempts may be hampered by this seclusion.

Getting Rid of Tramadol's Hold In order to recover from tramadol dependence, one must treat the psychological as well as the physical components of addiction.

Among the solutions are
Therapeutic interventions include therapy and counseling to deal with underlying emotional problems.

Support groups: A forum for peers to exchange experiences and provide empathy.

Creating non-pharmaceutical coping mechanisms to handle emotional discomfort is known as healthy coping.

The pitfalls of drug addiction are starkly shown by the trap associated with tramadol. We can enable young people to break out from the cycle and regain their emotional resilience by educating them about the psychological effects of tramadol abuse and providing all-inclusive remedies.

CHAPTER 4

BEYOND COMMON SUBSTANCES

Lesser-Known Drugs and Their Psychological Impact

Although marijuana and tramadol are often the focus of conversations about drug addiction in young people, there are several more lesser-known drugs that may be just as harmful, if not more, to young people's mental health. These drugs and their significant influence on the developing mind are discussed in this chapter.

The Dunesome World of Designer Substances Synthetic medications, also referred to as designer drugs, are made to replicate the effects of well-known substances. Because of their ability to dodge legal limits and their constantly changing chemical configurations, they often go unnoticed. Examples include artificial cathinones (also known as **"bath salts")** and synthetic cannabinoids (sometimes known as **"spice"**).

The Effects of Synthetic Drugs on the Mind.
Because these medicines are strong and uncontrolled, their psychological effects may be severe and unpredictable.

1.From Euphoria to Despair: Although there is an initial surge of extreme pleasure, there may be a subsequent decline that results in profound despair and thoughts of suicide.

2.Cognitive Disruption: There may be substantial impairments to learning, memory, and executive functioning.

3.Psychotic Session Duration
Hallucinations, paranoia, and delusions may be brought on by high dosages or continuous usage.

Prescription Medicine's Allure Misuse of prescription drugs is another issue that is becoming more and more problematic. Addiction to anxiety, ADHD, and sleep disorders medications may result in:

1.Dependency: The psychological need for medicine to maintain regular bodily functions.

2.Withdrawal: During withdrawal phases, there may be significant anxiety, mood fluctuations, and cognitive loss.

The Increase in Nootropic Use Nootropics, also known as "smart drugs," are compounds that make the promise to improve cognitive abilities.

Off-label usage by young people pursuing academic or professional benefits may result in the following outcomes, even if some are legal and utilized for medical conditions:

1.Unrealistic Expectations: Substance abuse as a means of improving cognition.

2.Risks to Mental Health: Possible aggravation of preexisting mental health conditions.

Finding My Way Through the Unknown These compounds are especially harmful due to their unexpected nature. Among the ways to lessen their influence are:

1.**Regulation and monitoring:** Keeping up with new medication developments and revising legislation.

2.**Teaching and Raising Awareness** Teaching young people about the dangers of these drugs.

3.Access to Mental Health Services: Helping those who are suffering from negative psychological consequences.

There are many unknown medications in the wide and dangerous world of pharmaceuticals. We can better equip young people to make informed choices and seek assistance when necessary by bringing these drugs to light and talking about their psychological effects. This chapter is an invaluable resource for understanding and resolving the difficulties presented by the less well-known causes of drug addiction.

CHAPTER 5

THE DOWNWARD SPIRAL

Addiction and Mental Health Disorders

For many young people, the nexus of addiction and mental health issues is a dangerous place to be. This chapter explores the vicious cycle that connects drug addiction to mental health issues, weaving a complicated web that may trap a developing mind.

The Phenomenon of Co-occurrence Professionals refer to the co-occurrence of mental health issues and addiction as dual diagnosis.
Adolescents who are experiencing emotional distress may resort to drugs like tramadol or marijuana in an attempt to find momentary comfort, but this may quickly spiral out of control and worsen their mental health problems.

The Fall Commences Usually, social pressure, stress, or mental health issues lead to drug use that seems safe at first, which sets off the cycle. increasing tolerance and dependency result from changes in brain chemistry brought on by increasing usage.

Mental Health Conditions and Drug Abuse Addiction and mental health conditions that often co-occur together include:

1.Depression: A severe depressive state that may result in drug self-medication.

2.Anxiety disorders: Severe anxiety that drugs may be able to temporarily calm.

3.Bipolar Disorder: Severe mood fluctuations that may be misunderstood as being "regulated" by medication.

4.Post-Traumatic Stress Disorder (PTSD) Substance abuse-related symptoms of trauma that are often dulled.

The Effect on the Life of the Youth Wide-ranging are the effects of this downward spiral:

1.**Academic Decline**: Difficulty focusing or achieving academic success.

2.Loss of interest in once-enjoyed relationships and activities is known as social withdrawal.

3.**Health Deterioration**: There is a decline in both mental and physical health, as well as a higher chance of getting chronic illnesses.

Ending the Cycle It is possible to stop and turn around the spiral, but it will need a diverse strategy:

Integrated treatment aims to treat the mental health issue and addiction at the same time.

1.Support systems: Companion groups, family, and friends that provide encouragement and understanding.

2.Expert Assistance: availability of psychiatrists, counselors, and therapists with dual diagnosis expertise.

Comprehending the connection between mental health issues and addiction is essential for creating successful therapies. With the help of this chapter, young people and those who assist them should be able to identify the warning signals of a downward spiral and use the resources available to them to return to stability and health.

CHAPTER 6

BREAKING FREE

Psychological Approaches to Recovery

It takes bravery, dedication, and a thorough grasp of the psychological foundations of addiction to walk the road of change that is drug addiction recovery. The psychological strategies that enable people to escape the grip of addiction are the main topic of this chapter.

The Significance of Understanding The first step in recovery is insight, or a deep comprehension of the unique tendencies and situations that contribute to drug abuse. By use of introspection and professional counseling, young people may identify the underlying reasons for their addiction, whether it managing stress, overcoming trauma, or giving in to peer pressure.

Behavior-Cognitive Therapy (CBT) CBT is a fundamental component of psychiatric healing, assisting people in recognizing and combating harmful thinking patterns and drug-related behaviors. Youths may better control urges and prevent relapse by adopting healthy thought patterns.

Conducting Motivational Interviews (MI) MI is a team-based method that increases a person's desire to change. Youths are given the opportunity to express their desire for change and take charge of their own rehabilitation via the use of open-ended questions, thoughtful listening, and affirmation.

Meditating and Being Mindful By encouraging people to be mindful and in the moment, mindfulness activities help people become less impulsive, which often results in drug abuse. By promoting serenity and equilibrium, meditation may help with emotional control and lessen the need for drugs as a crutch.

Peer assistance and group therapy A forum for exchanging experiences and learning from others traveling similar pathways is offered by group therapy. Peer support groups, like 12-step programs, provide the feeling of responsibility and community that is essential for long-term recovery.

Family Consultation Relationships damaged by addiction may be repaired by including the family in the healing process. In addition to addressing the variables that may encourage drug use, family therapy fosters a nurturing atmosphere at home.

Preventing Relapses In order to stay sober, relapse prevention techniques are crucial. Teens acquire the ability to identify high-risk circumstances and acquire coping mechanisms so they may get through them without using drugs.

In order to overcome addiction, a person must work in concert with their loved ones, specialists, and themselves. Through the use of these psychological strategies, young people may recover from addiction and start a rewarding path toward long-term recovery.

CHAPTER 7

COMMUNITY AND SUPPORT

The Role of Peers and Family in Healing

The community and family are vital sources of support and safety for young people navigating the journey to overcome addiction.This chapter emphasizes how important these support networks are to the recovery process and how they may change lives.

The Peer-Healing Circle

Peer assistance is essential to the healing process. When young people confide in others who have had similar problems, they often feel less alone and more understood. Recovery circles and other school-based programs are examples of peer-led support groups that provide a secure environment for candid conversation and supportive interaction.

Family: The Foundational Support System The most important person in a young person's healing process may be their family. Healing begins with a healthy family setting that promotes understanding, candid conversation, and unconditional love. Sessions of family therapy may aid in restoring trust and healing the emotional wounds brought on by addiction.

The Function of the Community

A nurturing community provides chances for personal development, resources, and guidance, serving as an extended family. Youths need a feeling of purpose and connection to sustain sobriety; community centers, neighborhood health services, and volunteer groups may help.

Educational Establishments as Activators Universities and schools are in a unique position to positively impact young people. Educational institutions may take the lead in preventing addiction and assisting students in recovery by putting in place thorough drug education programs and offering counseling services.

Positive Role Models' Effects

Teenagers might be motivated to choose a drug-free lifestyle by mentors and role models in the community. These people provide insight and counsel gleaned from their experiences, demonstrating that there are options in life outside of addiction.

Creating a Support Network Building a strong support system entails:

Engaging Local Leaders: Including prominent members of the community in rehabilitation and awareness initiatives.

Encouraging kids to engage in community service as a means of building self-worth and empathy.

Ensuring kids have easy access to mental health treatments and recreational opportunities is part of facilitating their access to resources.

Peers, families, and the community work together to create a web of support that may help lift young people out of the shadow of addiction. In the fight against drug addiction, this chapter emphasizes the need for a unified front and the fact that recovery is a journey that is best undertaken in tandem.

CHAPTER 8

A NEW DAWN

Life Beyond Addiction

The shadow of addiction may fade and expose the promise of a new day, just as the blackness of the night gives way to the first rays of dawn.

The chance for people to find themselves free from the mask of drug abuse is sometimes referred to as the Rebirth of Self Recovery. This is a chance for young people to discover and pursue interests, skills, and goals that were previously obscured by addiction.

The Healing of Connections

Although addiction may weaken relationships with friends and family, recovery offers an opportunity to heal these links. After addiction, restoring connections and regaining trust are essential to leading a secure and caring life.

The Search for a Goal

Sobriety brings clarity, and purpose-seeking follows with clarity. Now that they are free from the bonds of addiction, young people may create objectives and work assiduously toward them. A new meaning is given to education, profession, and personal growth.

The Gratitude of Participation
The capacity to make a positive contribution to society is among the most satisfying parts of living a life free from addiction. Young people may become active members of their communities, mentors to those who are still in recovery, and champions for sobriety.

The Range of Services
The road to recovery never ends, even if the severe stage of addiction may have passed. Youths are kept attentive and resilient against the likelihood of relapse by ongoing treatment, participation in support groups, and self-care routines.

The Anniversary of Significant Occasions
Every day in recovery is an accomplishment, and significant anniversaries call for celebration. Recognizing accomplishments strengthens resolve to be drug-free and motivates others to continue on their recovery journey.

A life free from addiction is an acceptance of all that life has to offer, not just the cessation of chemical use. This chapter shines a light on a new dawn for young people who are ready to live the fullness of life while in recovery. It is a beacon of hope.

CONCLUSION

Setting Out for a Better Future

As "From Highs To Healing " comes to an end, we take stock of the adventure we have been through together. The difficult terrain of addiction has been explored in this book, along with the psychological struggles that our children confront. Solutions and rehabilitation tactics have also been highlighted, providing rays of hope.

Knowledge Is Power Throughout our voyage, knowledge has served as our compass. Youths are better prepared to deal with the intricacies of addiction if they have a greater awareness of the psychological foundations of addiction, how to identify the signs and symptoms, and the effects of drugs like marijuana and tramadol.

The Community's Strength We have witnessed firsthand how important family, friends, and the community are to the recovery process. People may be lifted out of the depths of addiction and guided toward long-term recovery by the network of strength created by the combined support and shared experiences.

The Hope for Rejuvenation Instead of being a destination, recovery is an ongoing process of development and rejuvenation. It is a route that points away from the darkness of reliance and in the direction of a happy, fulfilling existence.

The Request for Action In order to combat drug addiction, everyone reading this book is encouraged to band together, including parents, educators, kids, and community leaders. It's an opportunity to create settings that encourage wise decisions, assist those undergoing treatment, and strive toward a day when drug misuse won't cloud our children's potential.

The Wish for the Future Let's continue spreading the word of hope and using the resources we have acquired as we end this chapter. Let us set out on a more promising path, one in which our children experience the positive effects of recovery and everyone who takes this brave path to sobriety may reach the top.

Acknowledgements

As we flip the last page of "From Highs To Healing ," I send my greatest thanks to everyone who has made this book possible.

We especially thank the families and communities that help young people on their sober journey. The foundation of recovery and change is your constant love and support.

I want to recognize the important role that educators, mentors, and activists play in guiding our young people away from the dangers of drug addiction. Your dedication to fostering a better future for the next generation is society's greatest gift.

We are all committed to the idea that every young person has the capacity to make a significant recovery and that recovery is achievable. This book is an ode to that conviction and all those who help to bring it to pass.